Artistic
MANDALAS

Stress-Relieving Designs: Mandalas, Flowers, Floral Patterns, Decorative Designs, Paisley Patterns

Monica Aryl-White

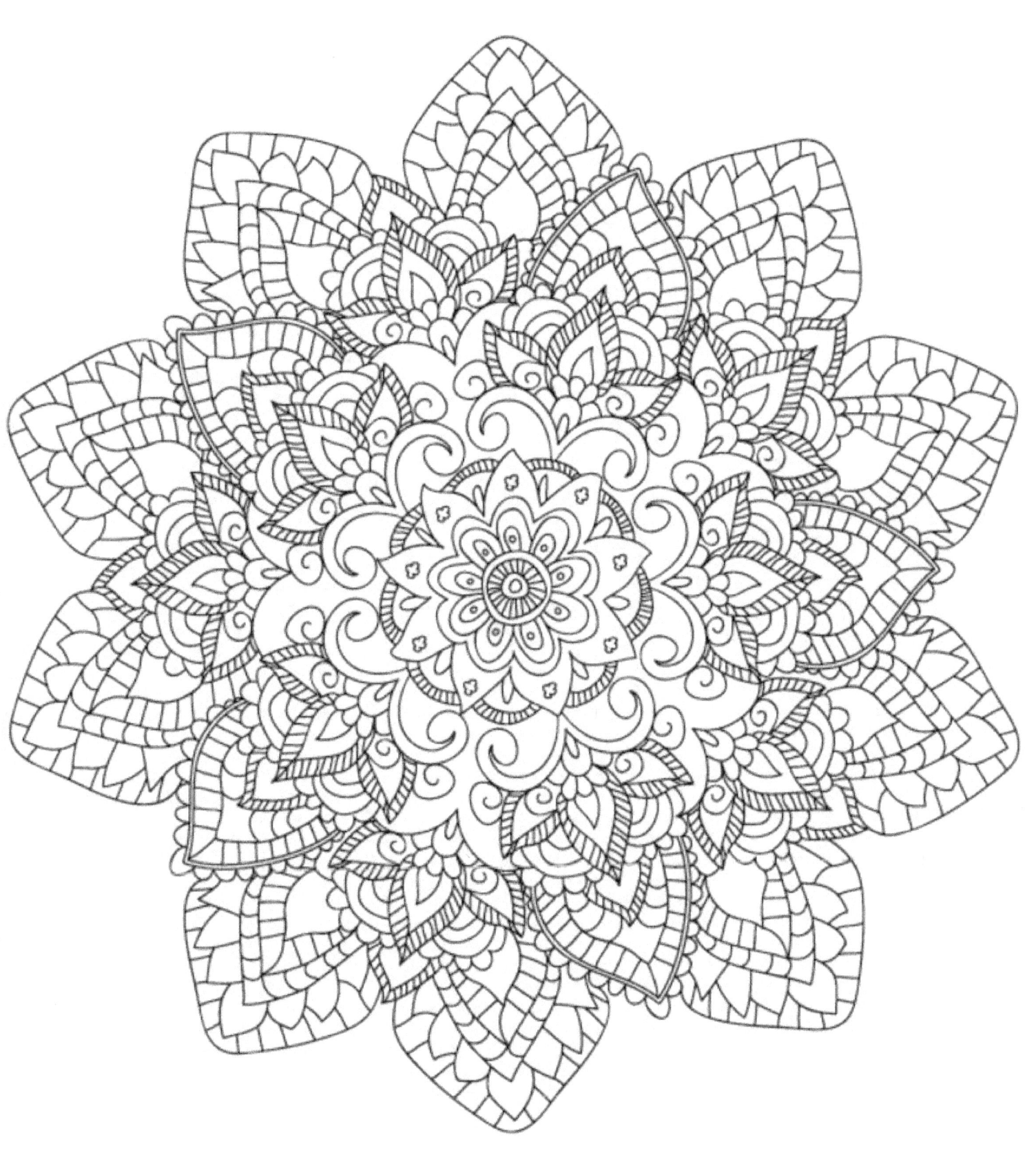

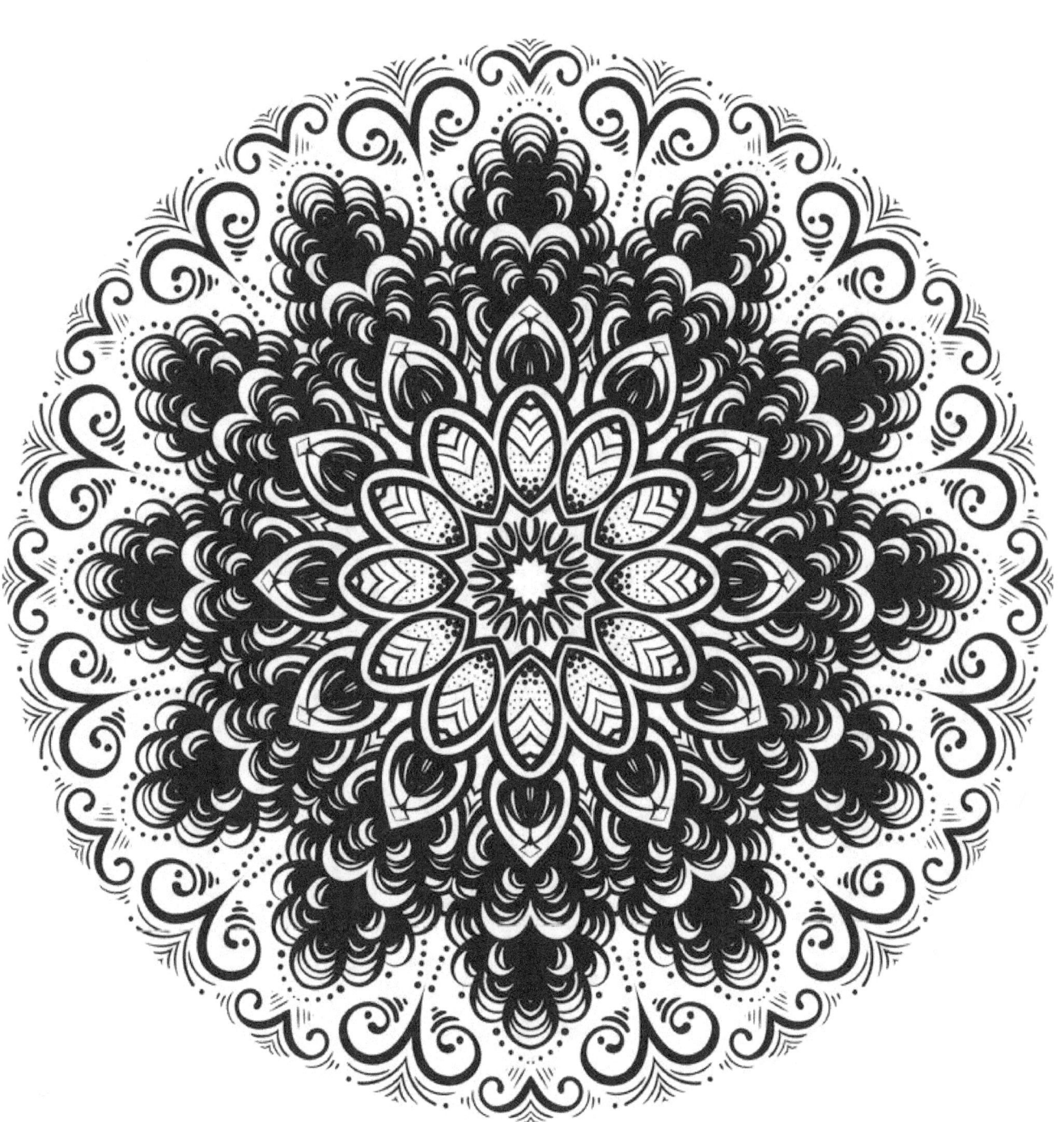

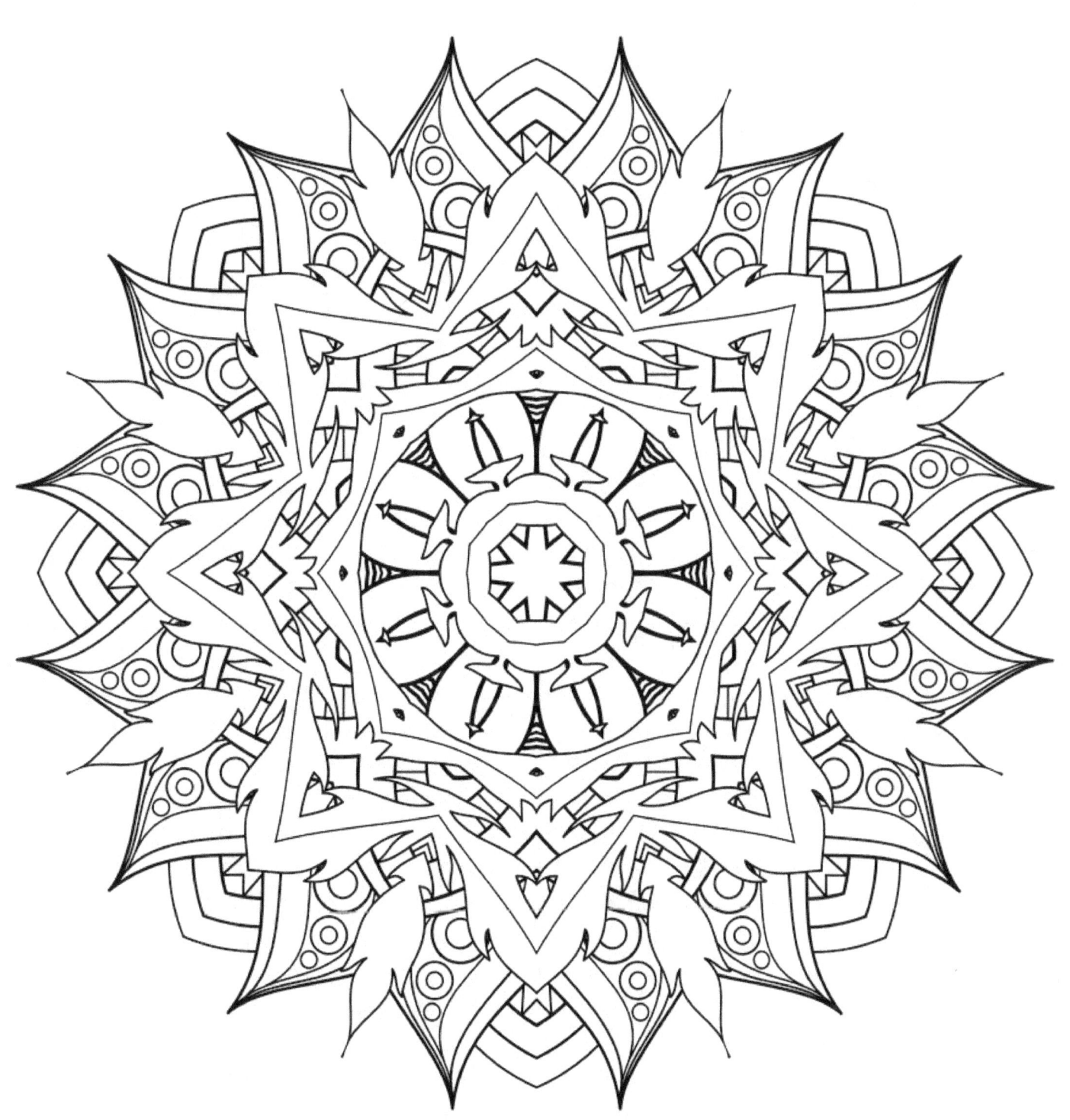

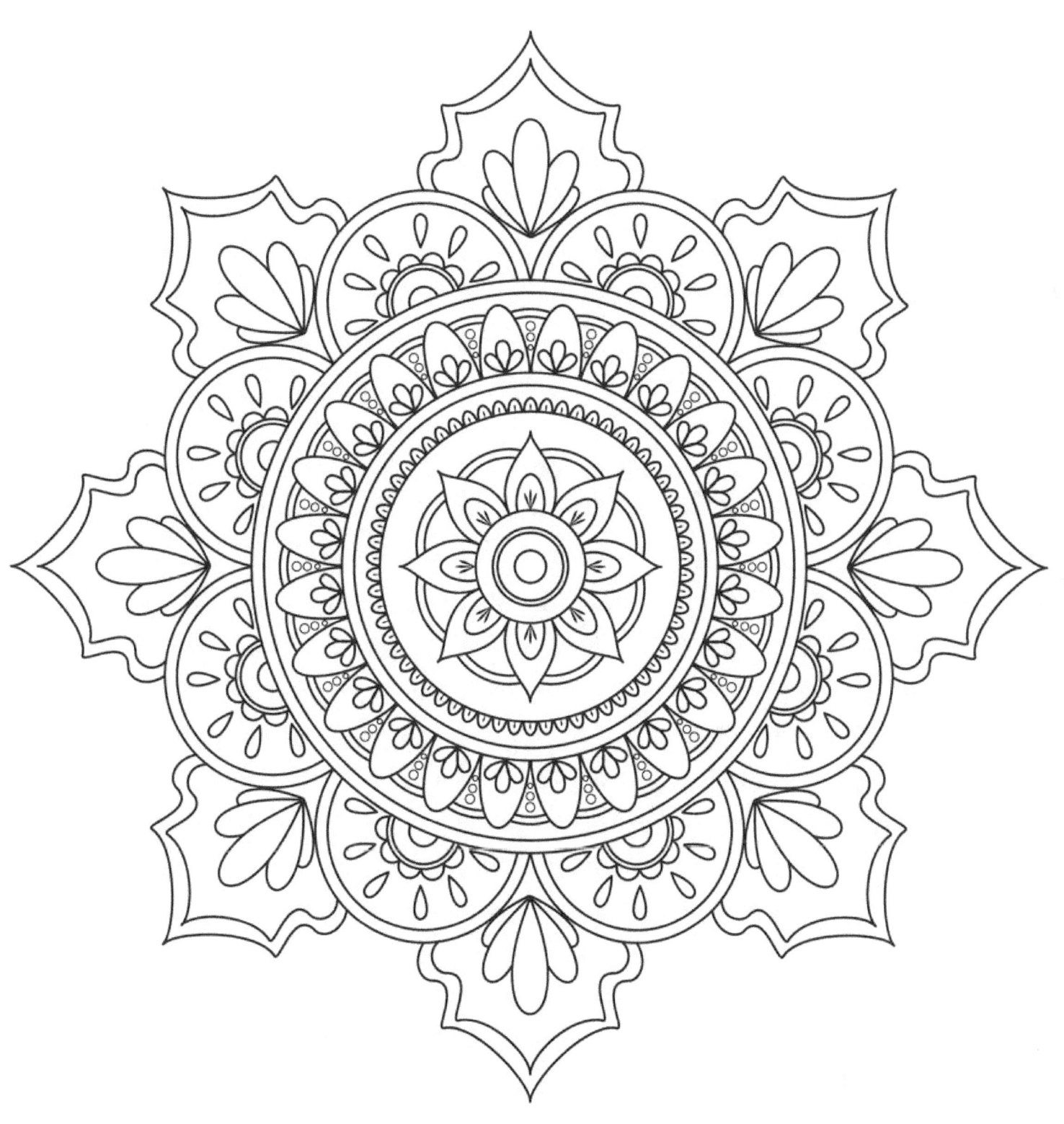

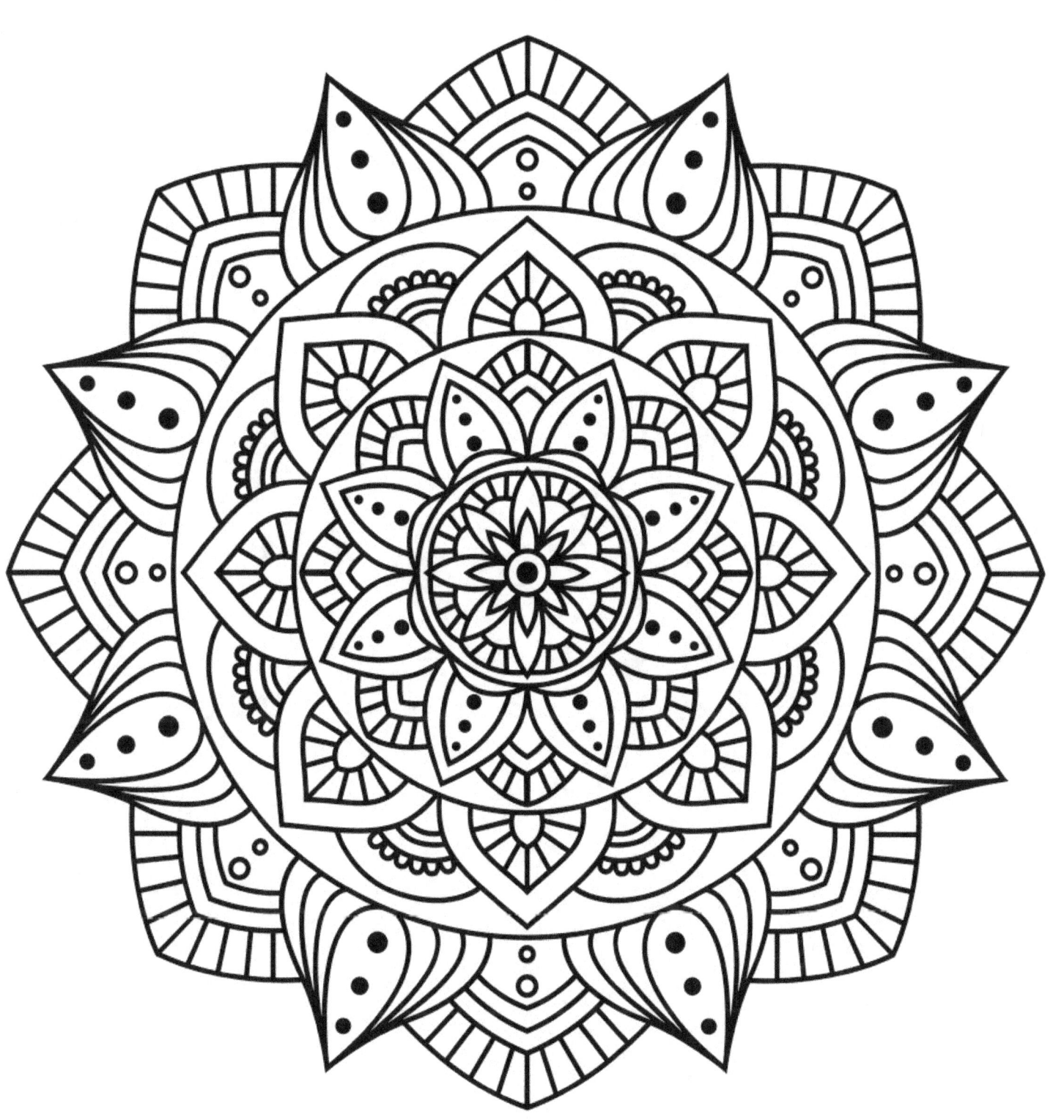

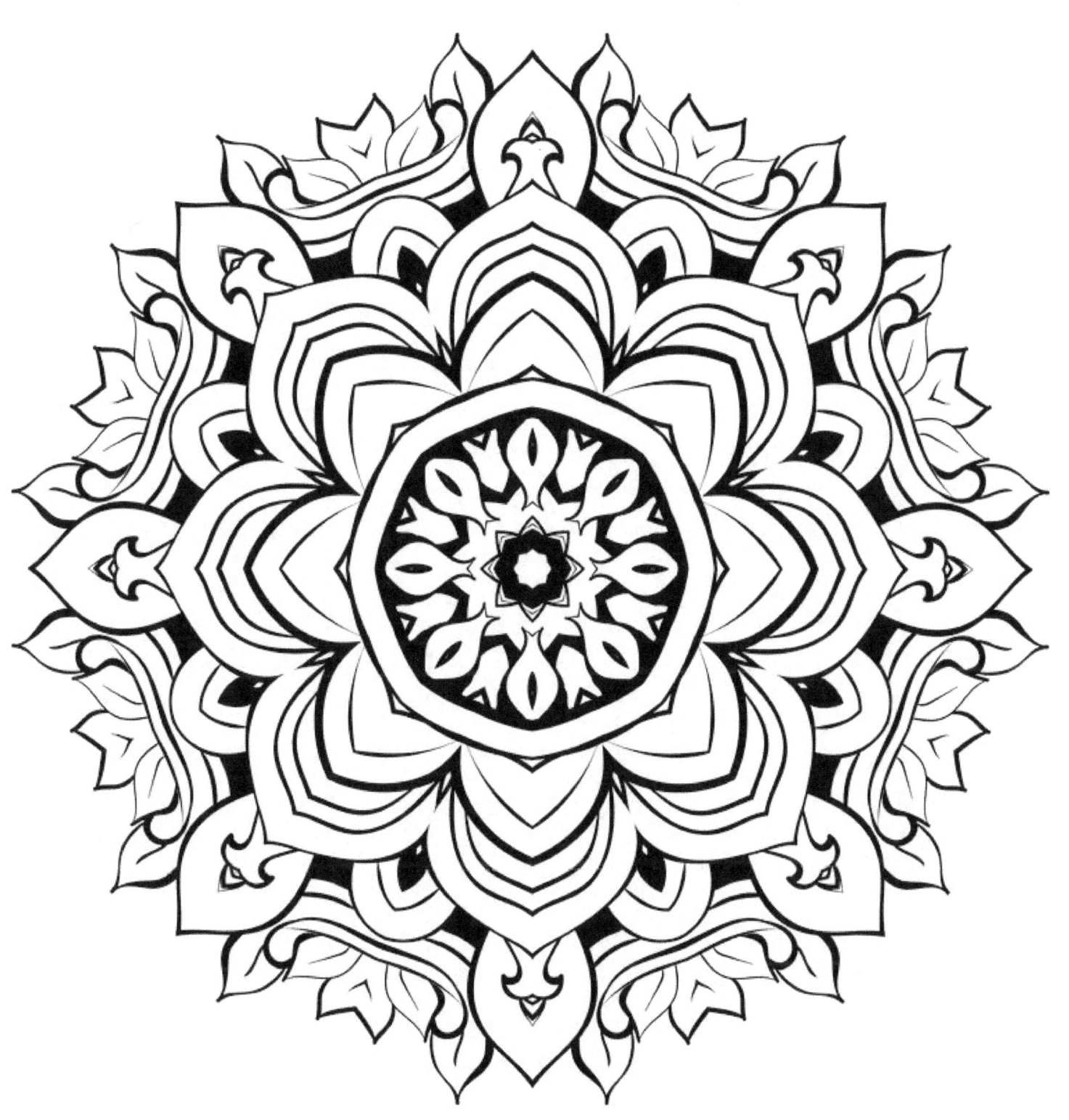

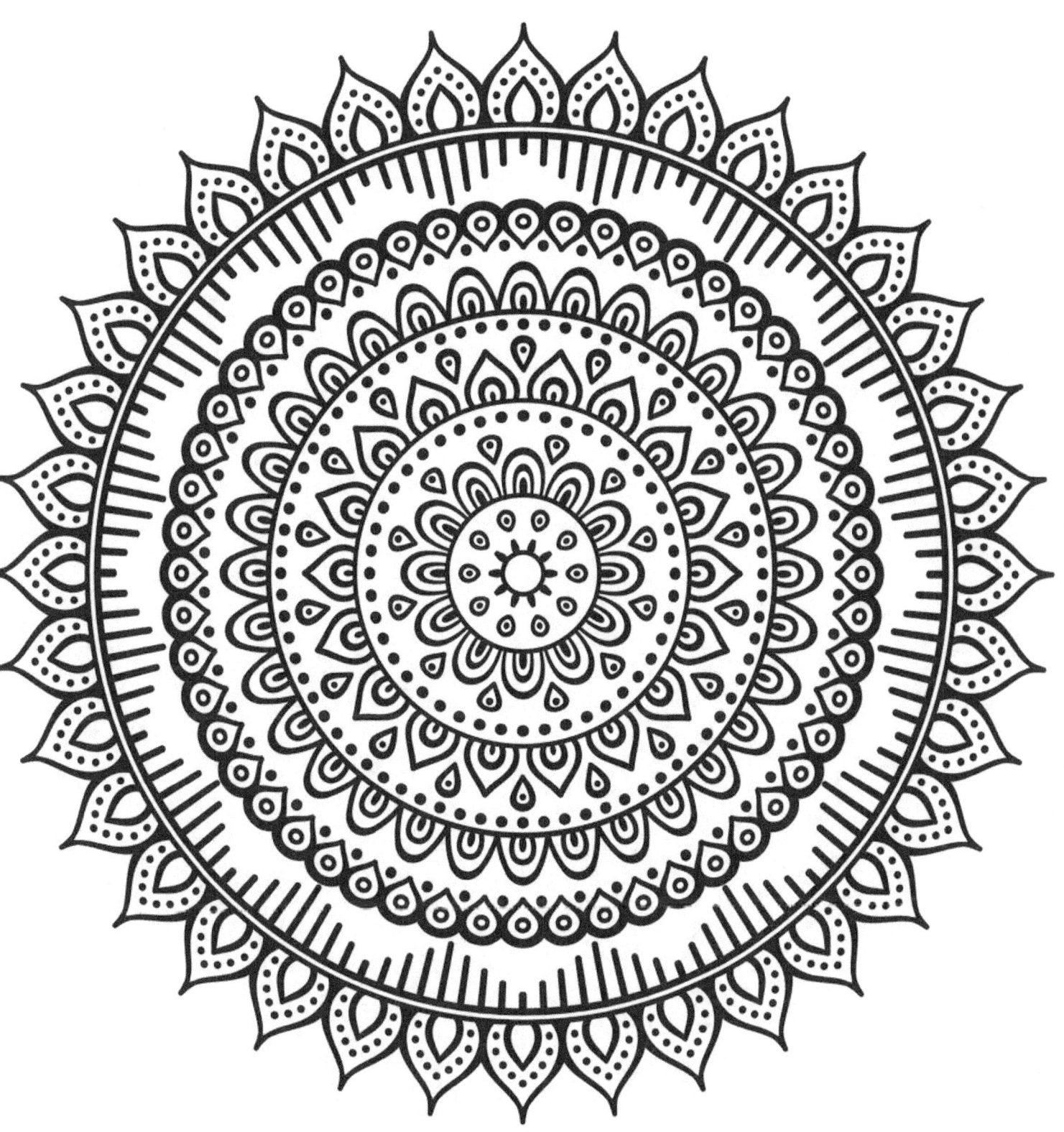

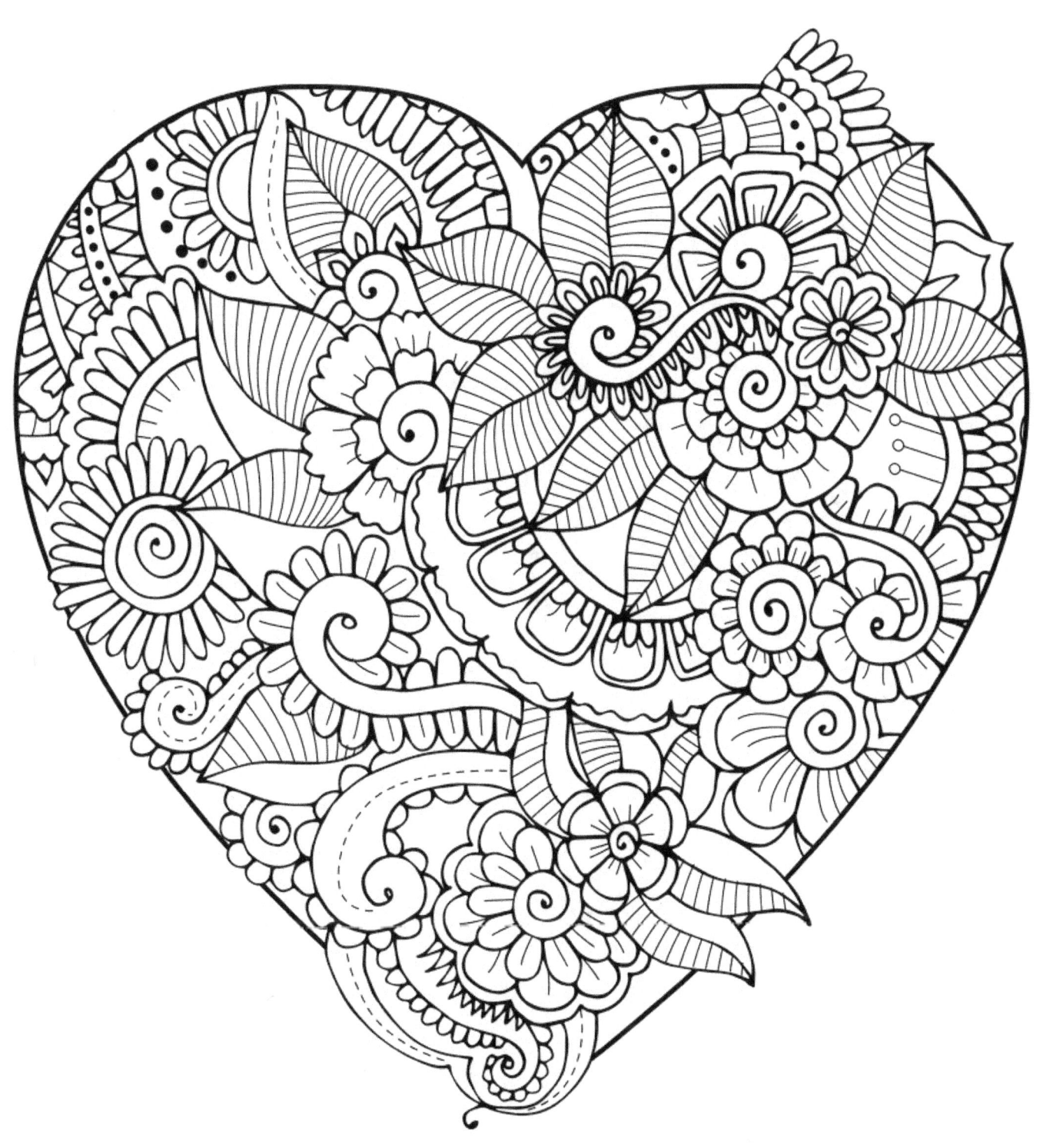

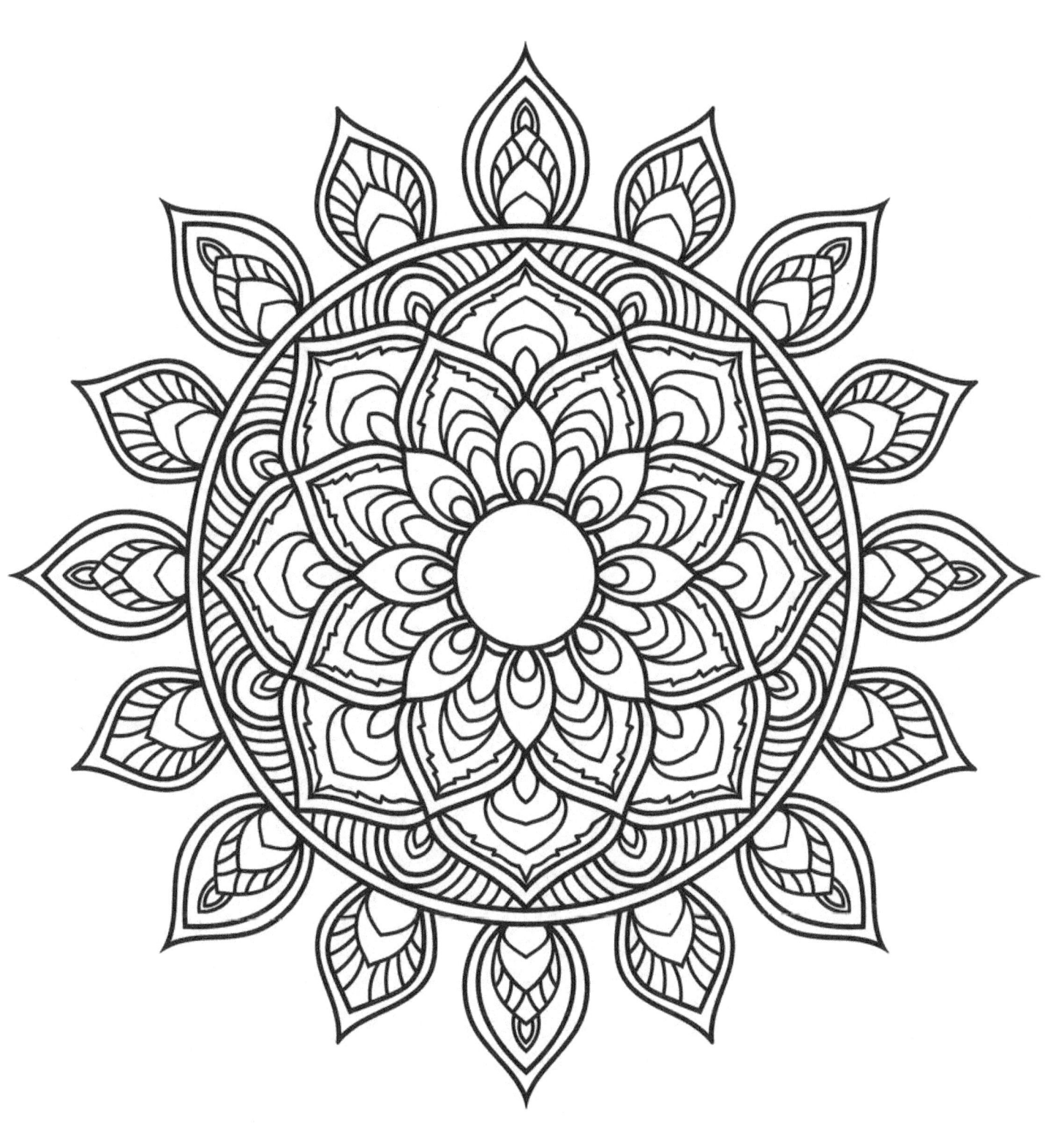

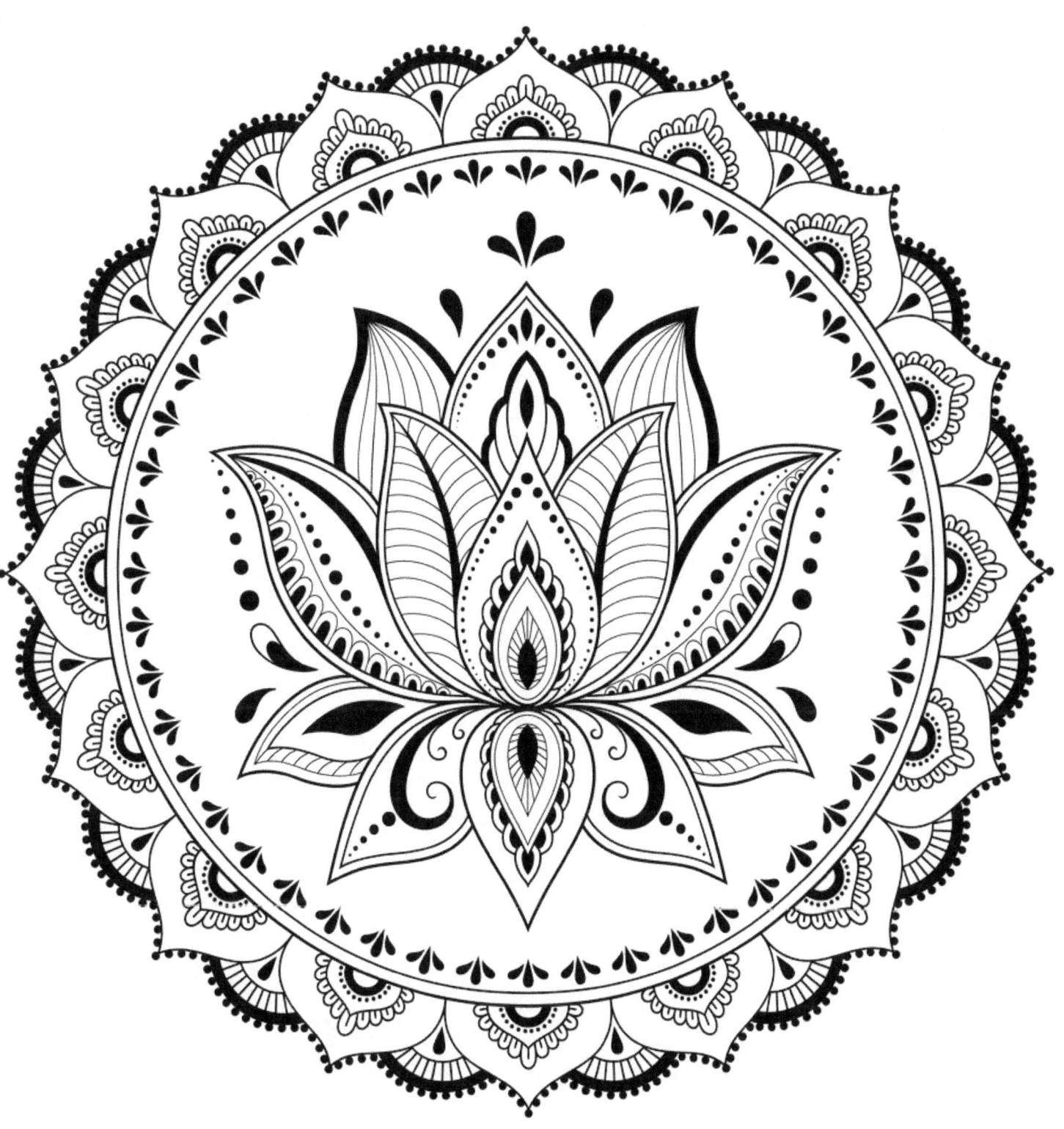

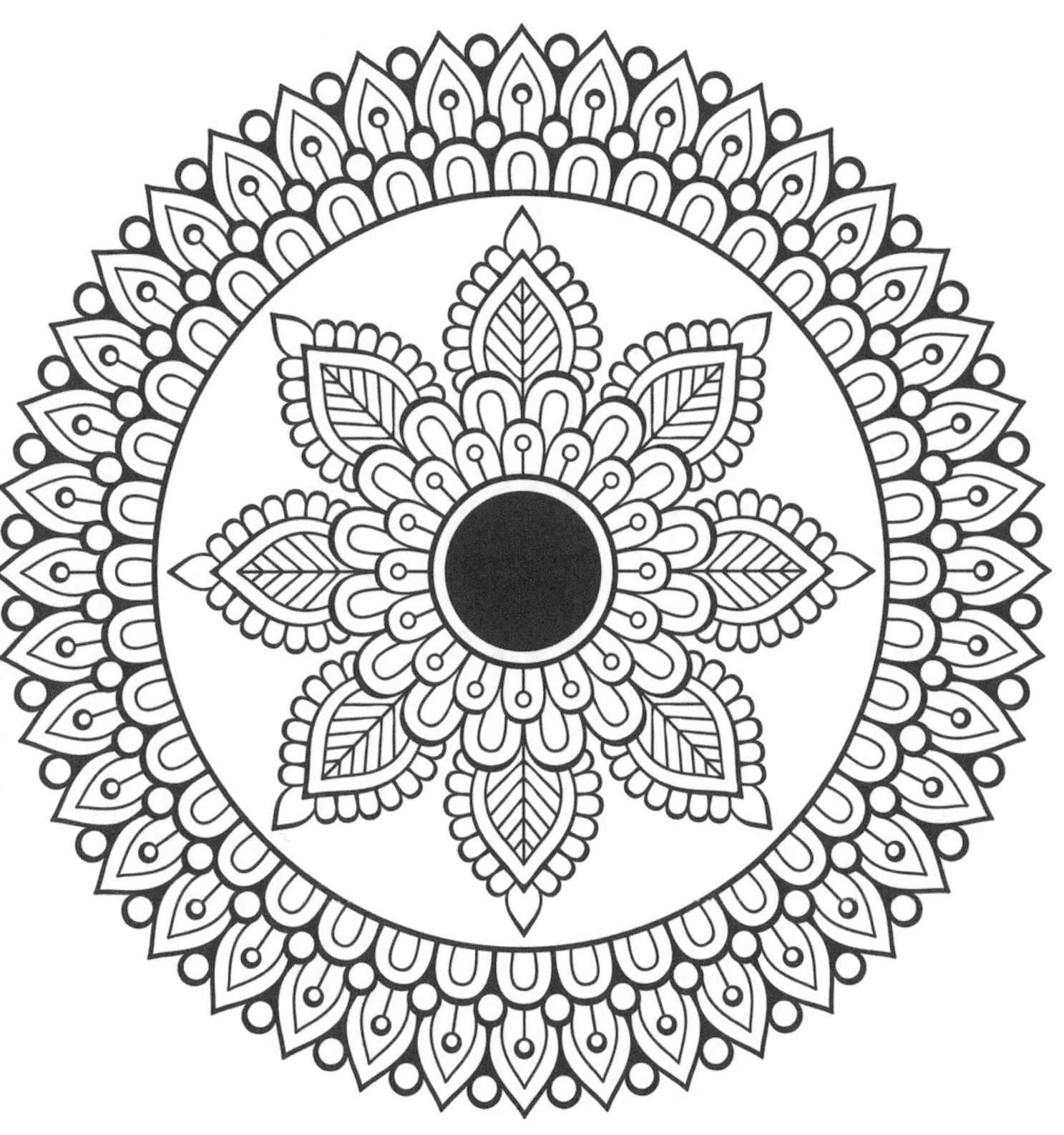

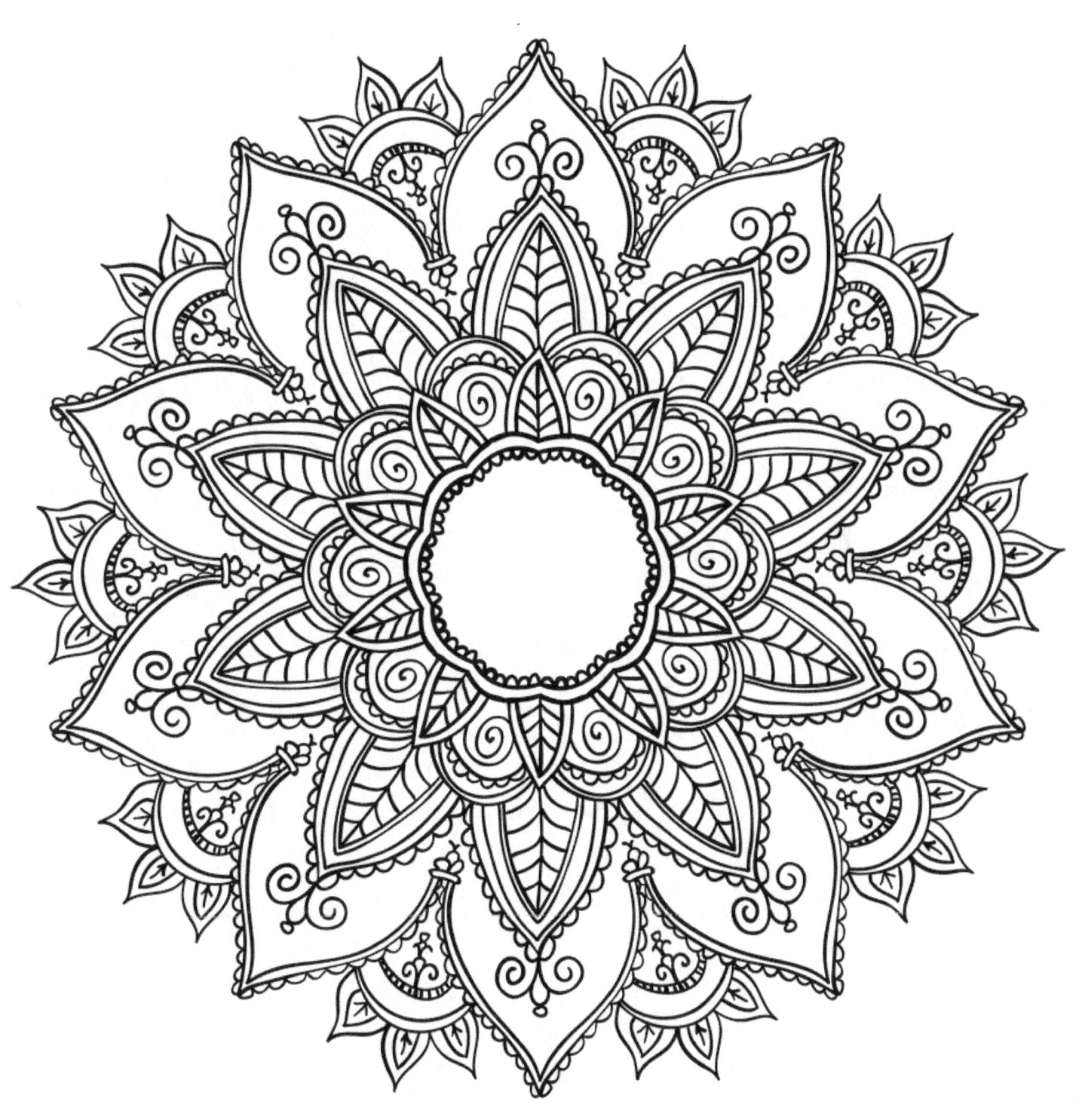

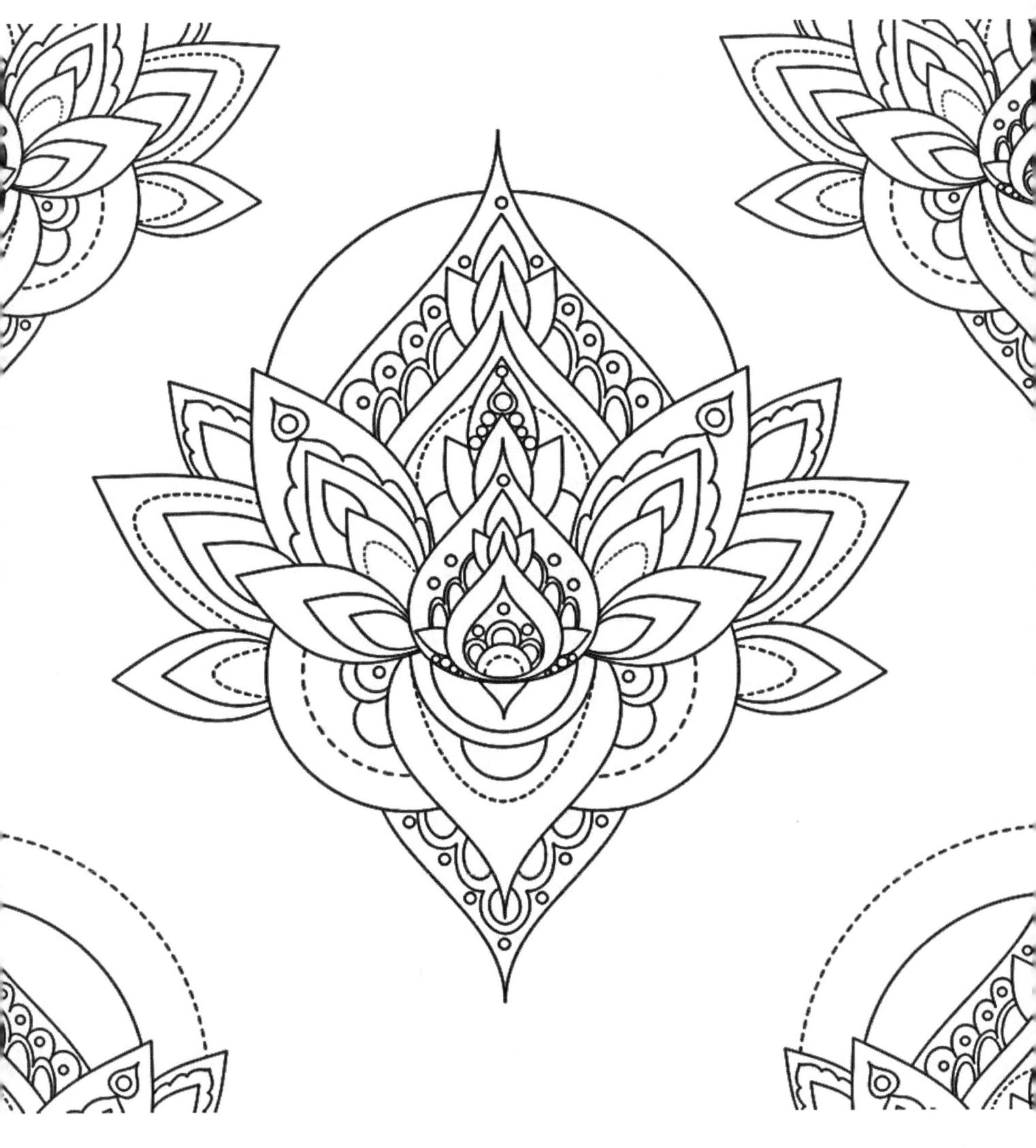

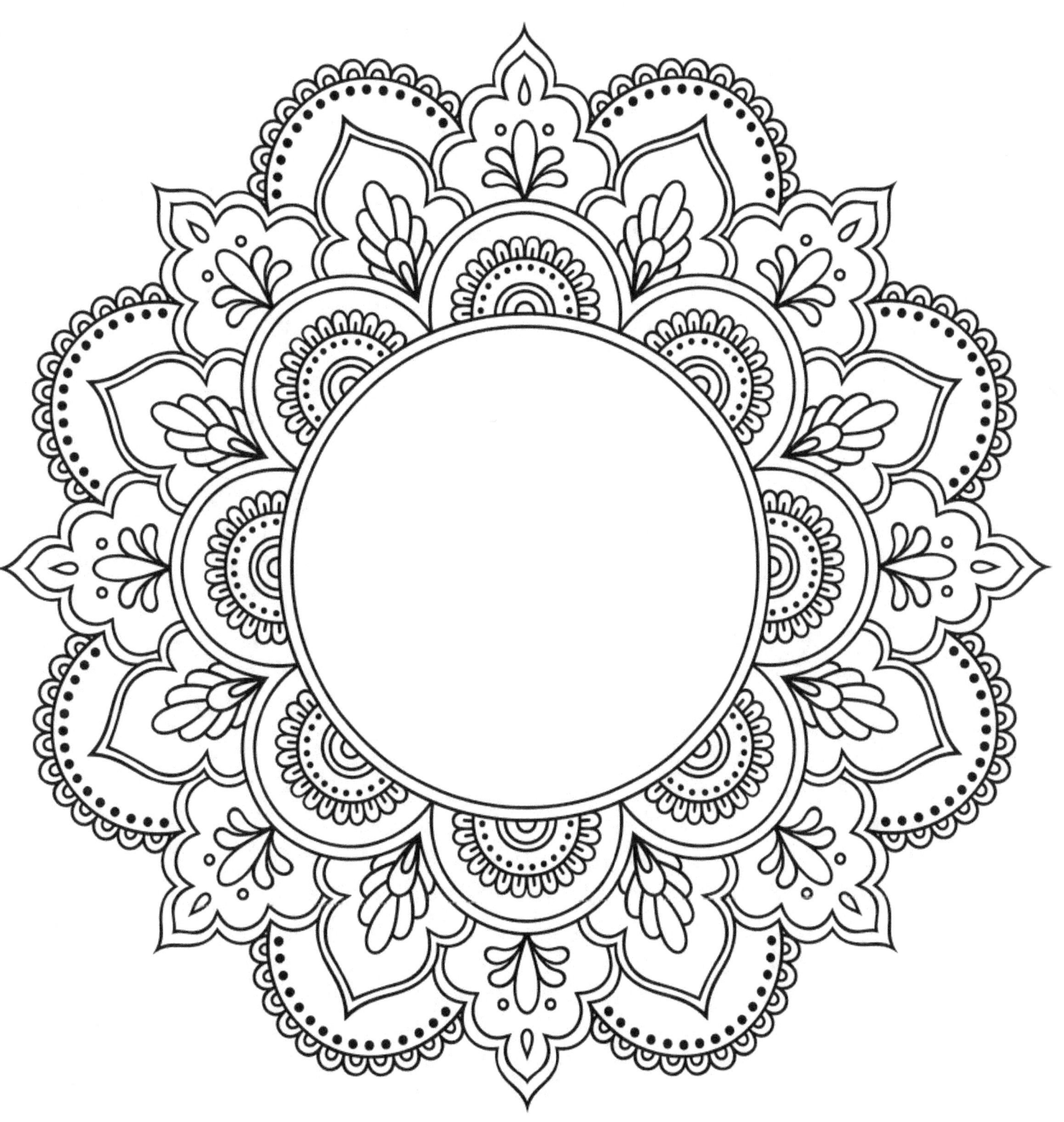

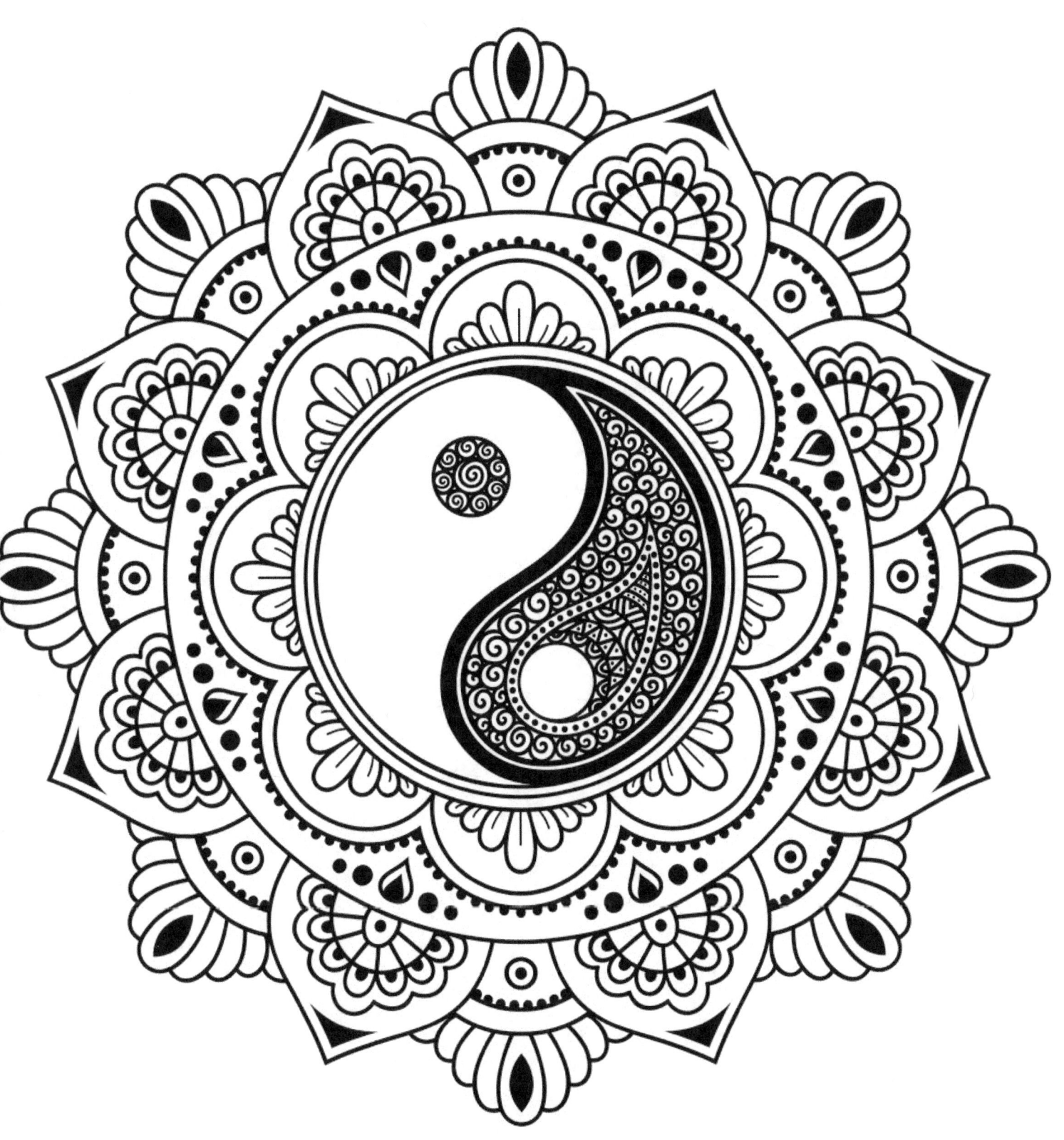

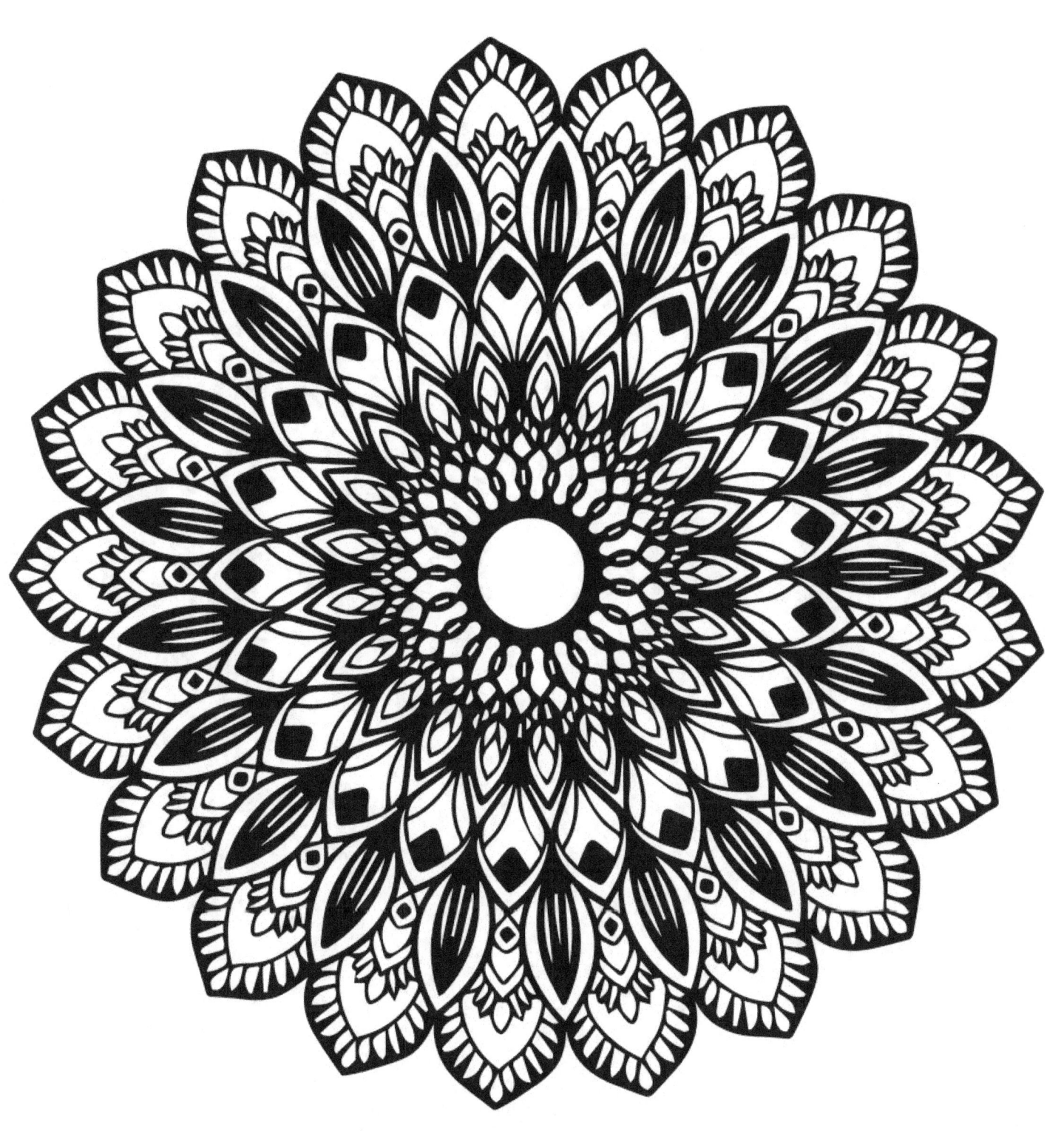

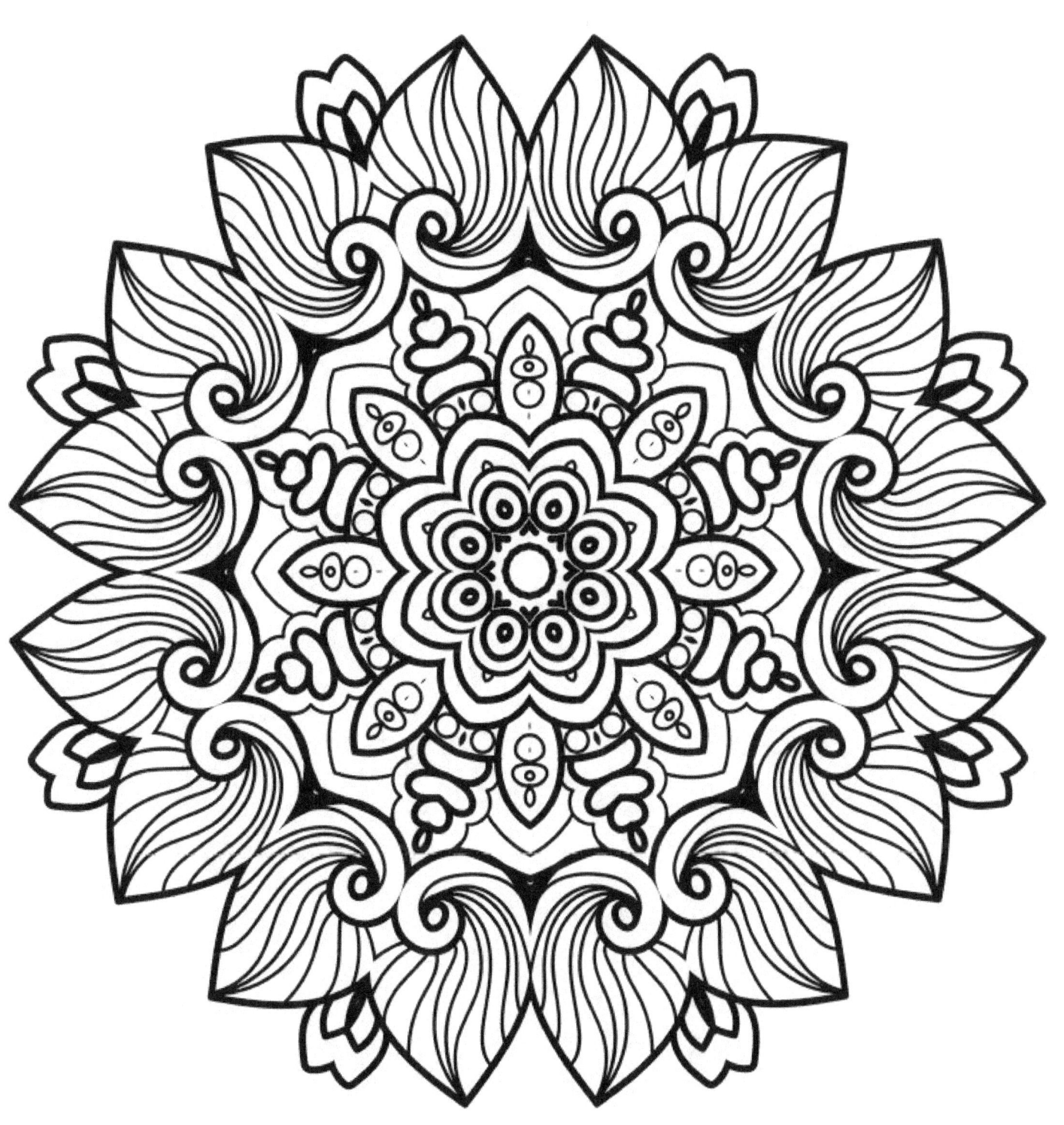

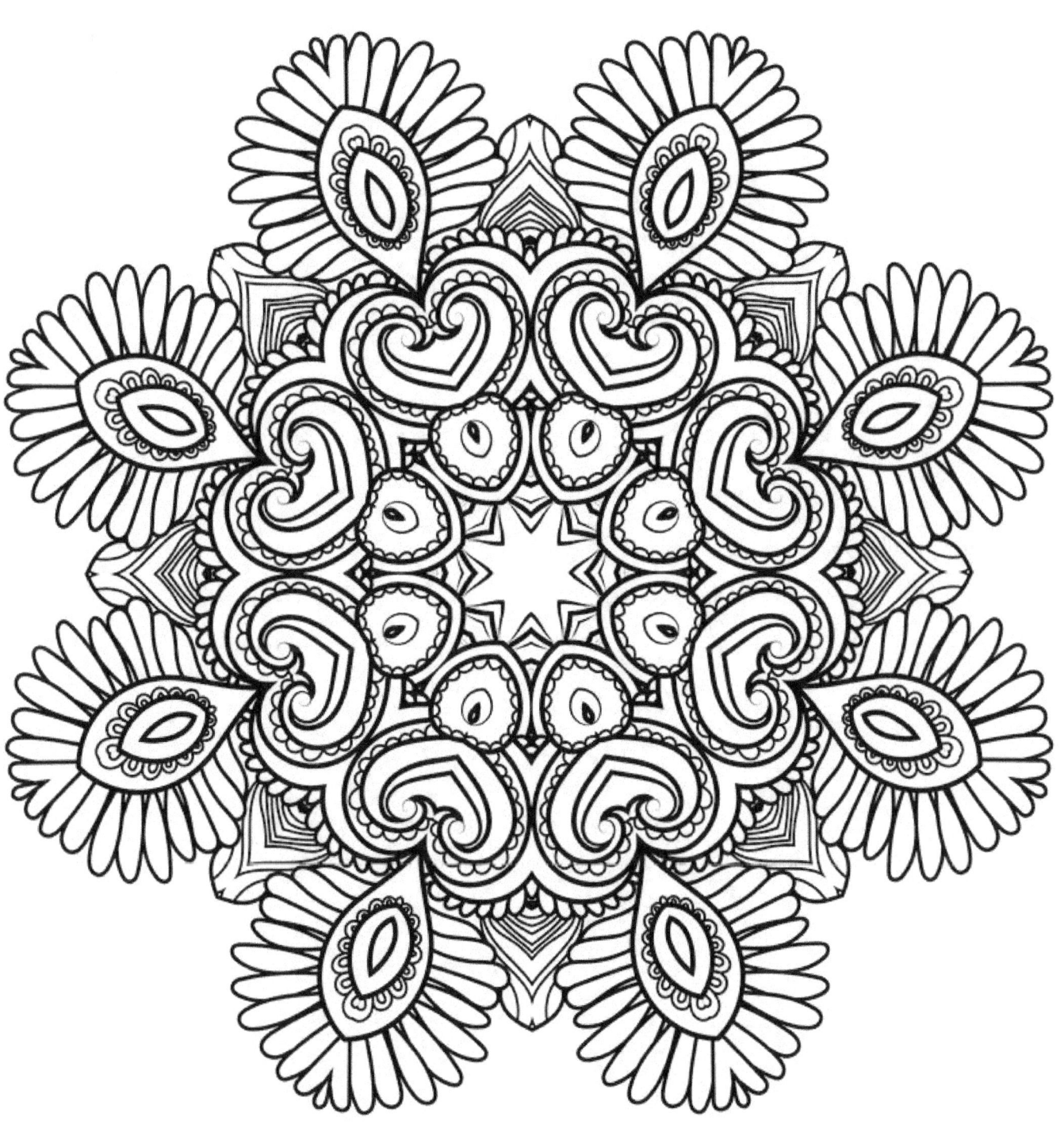

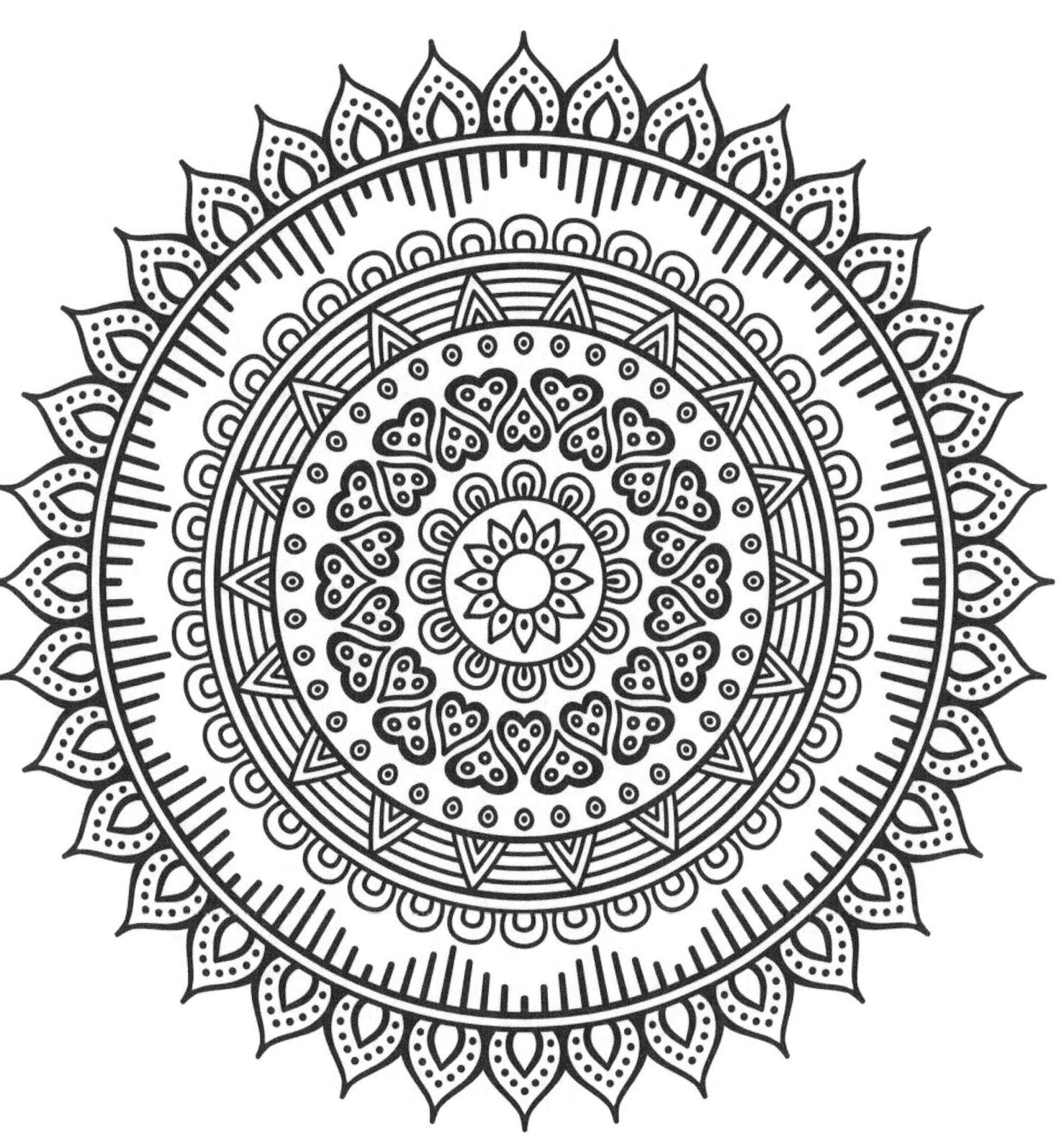

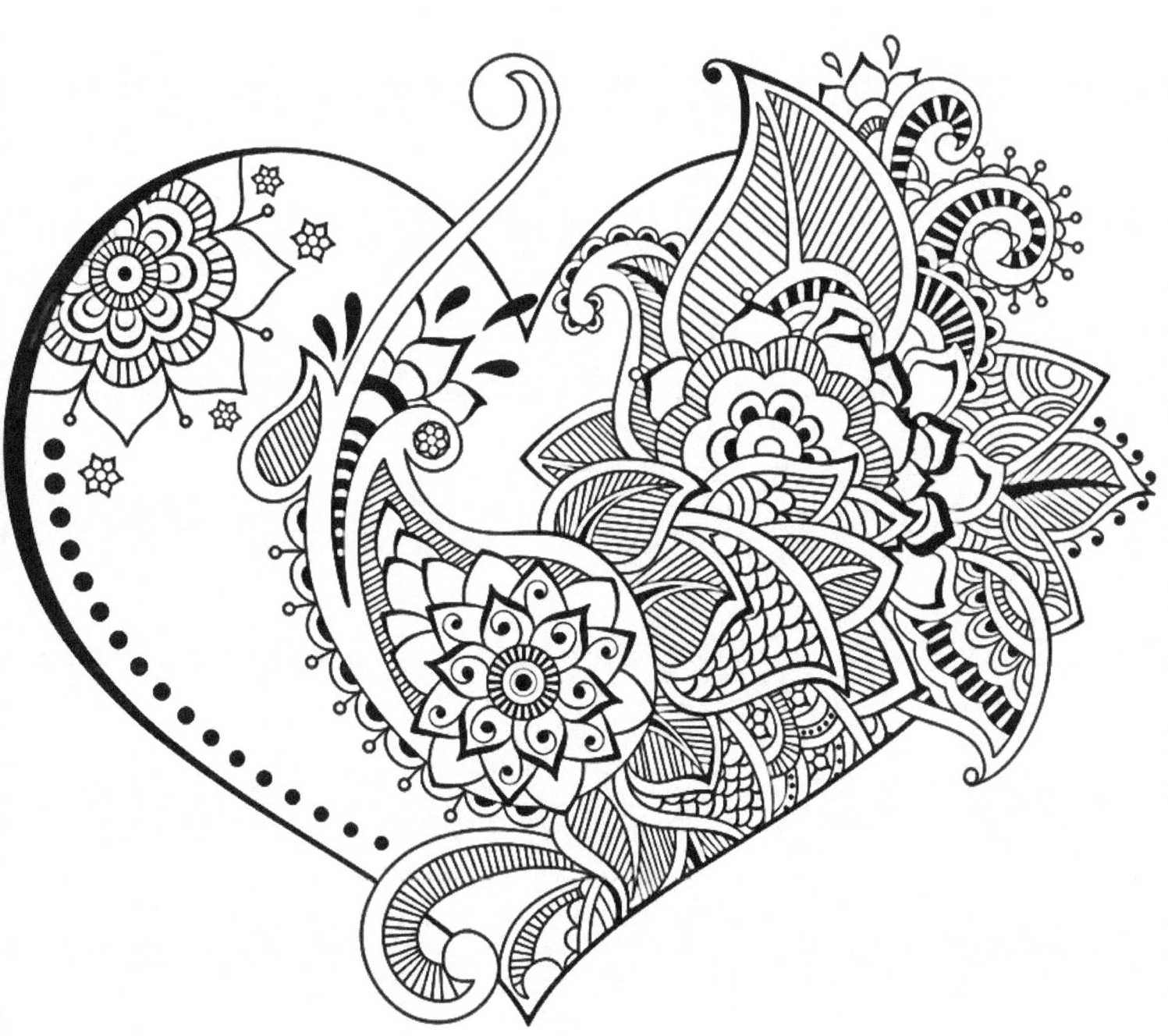

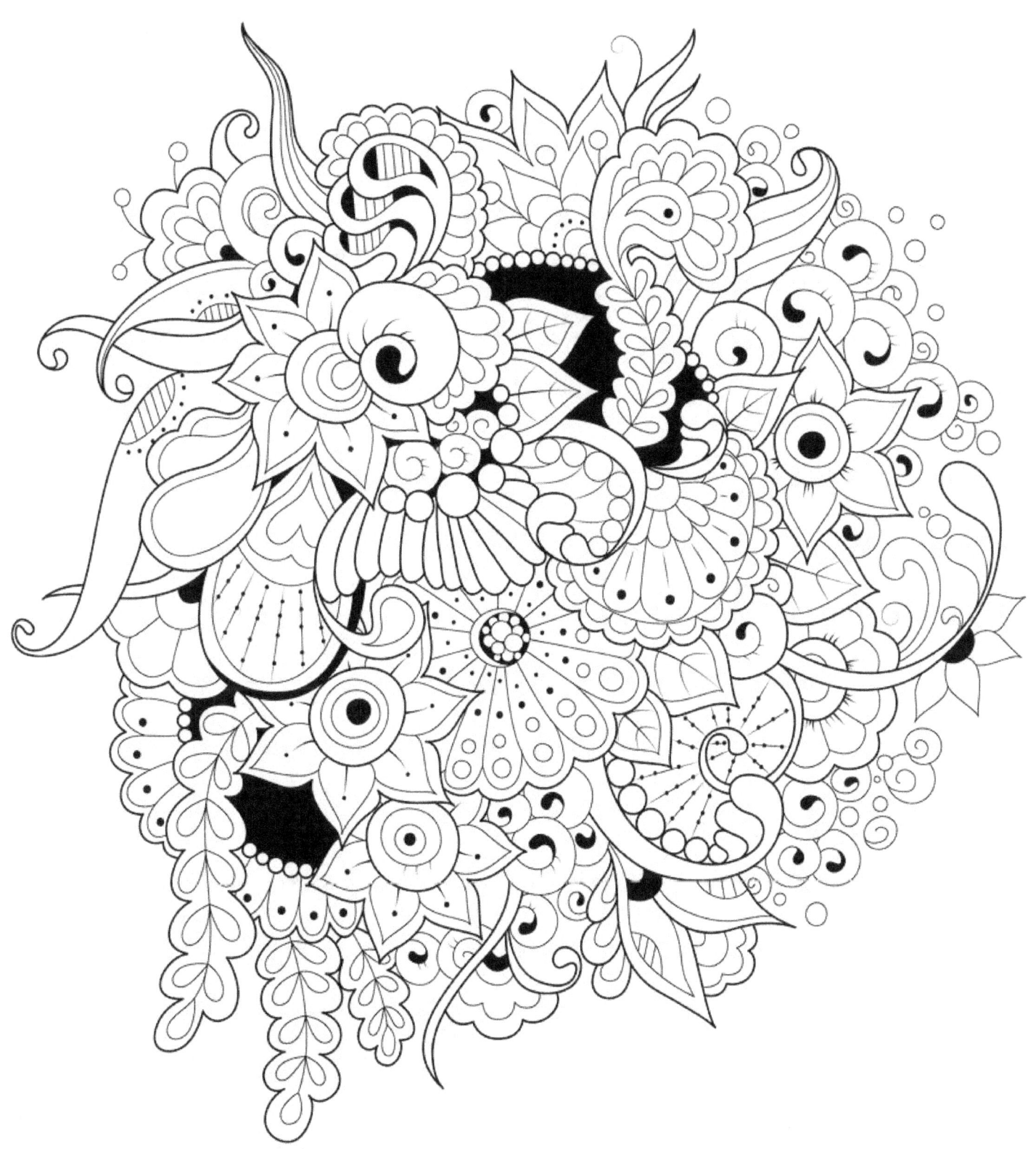

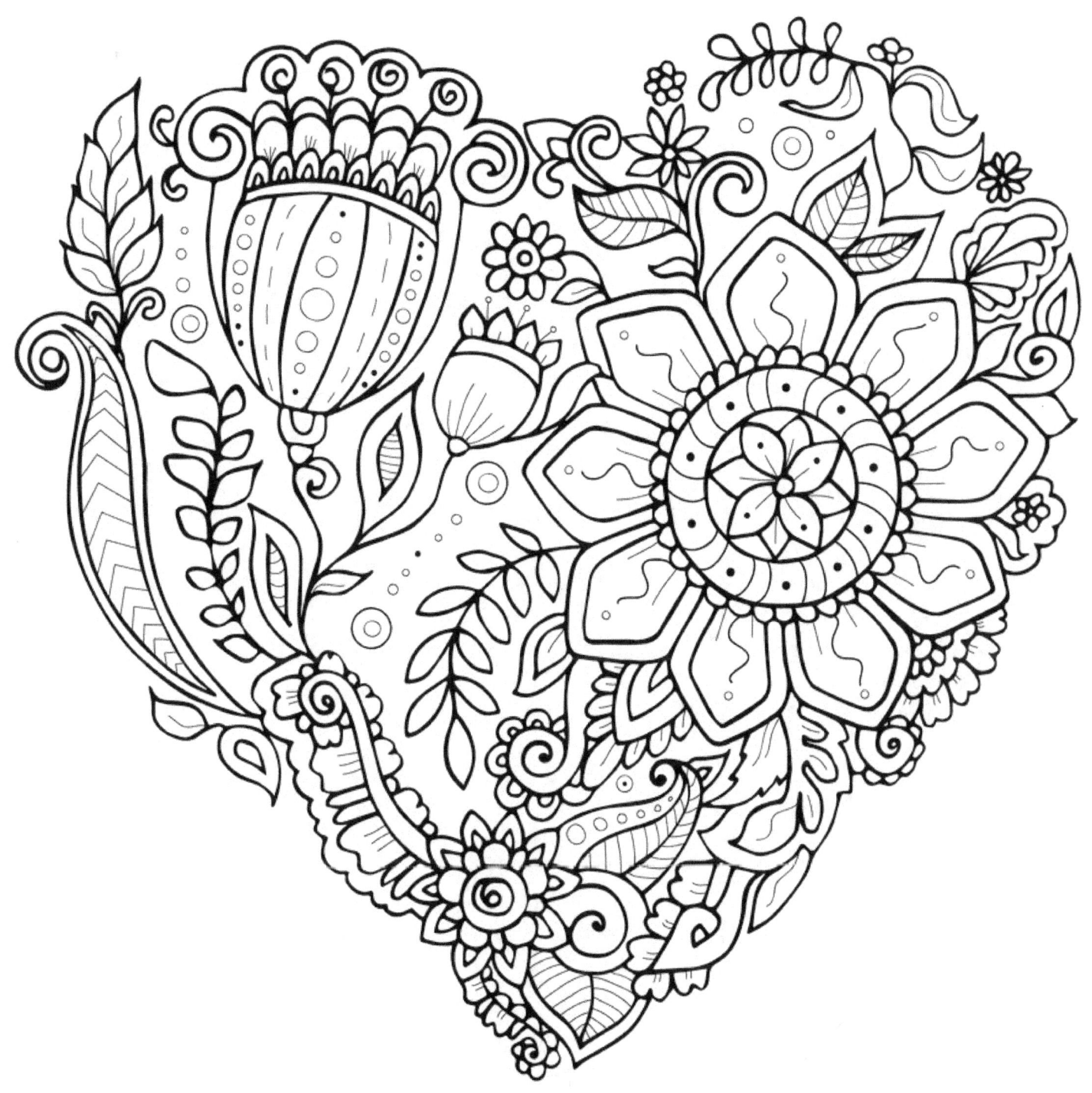

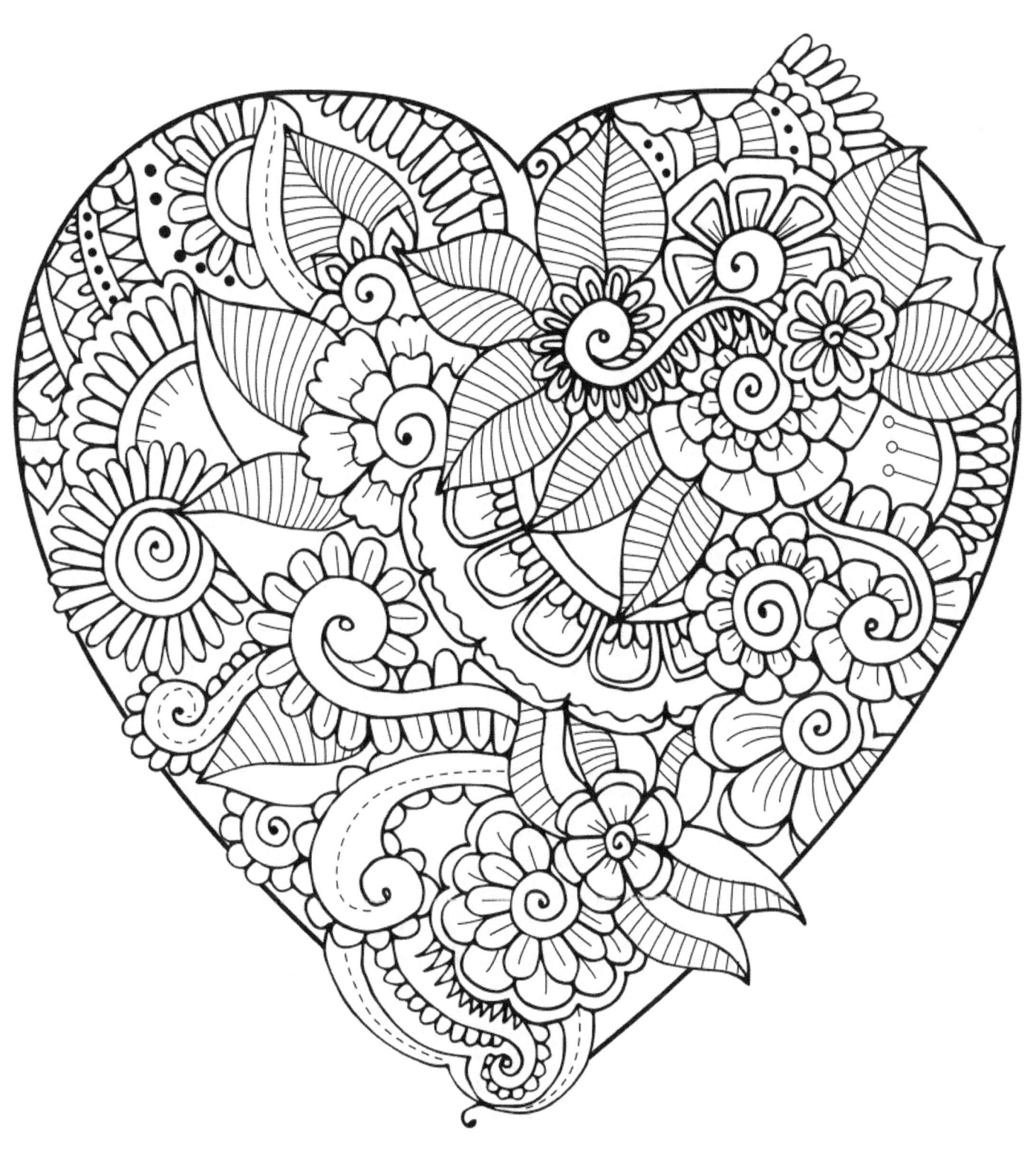

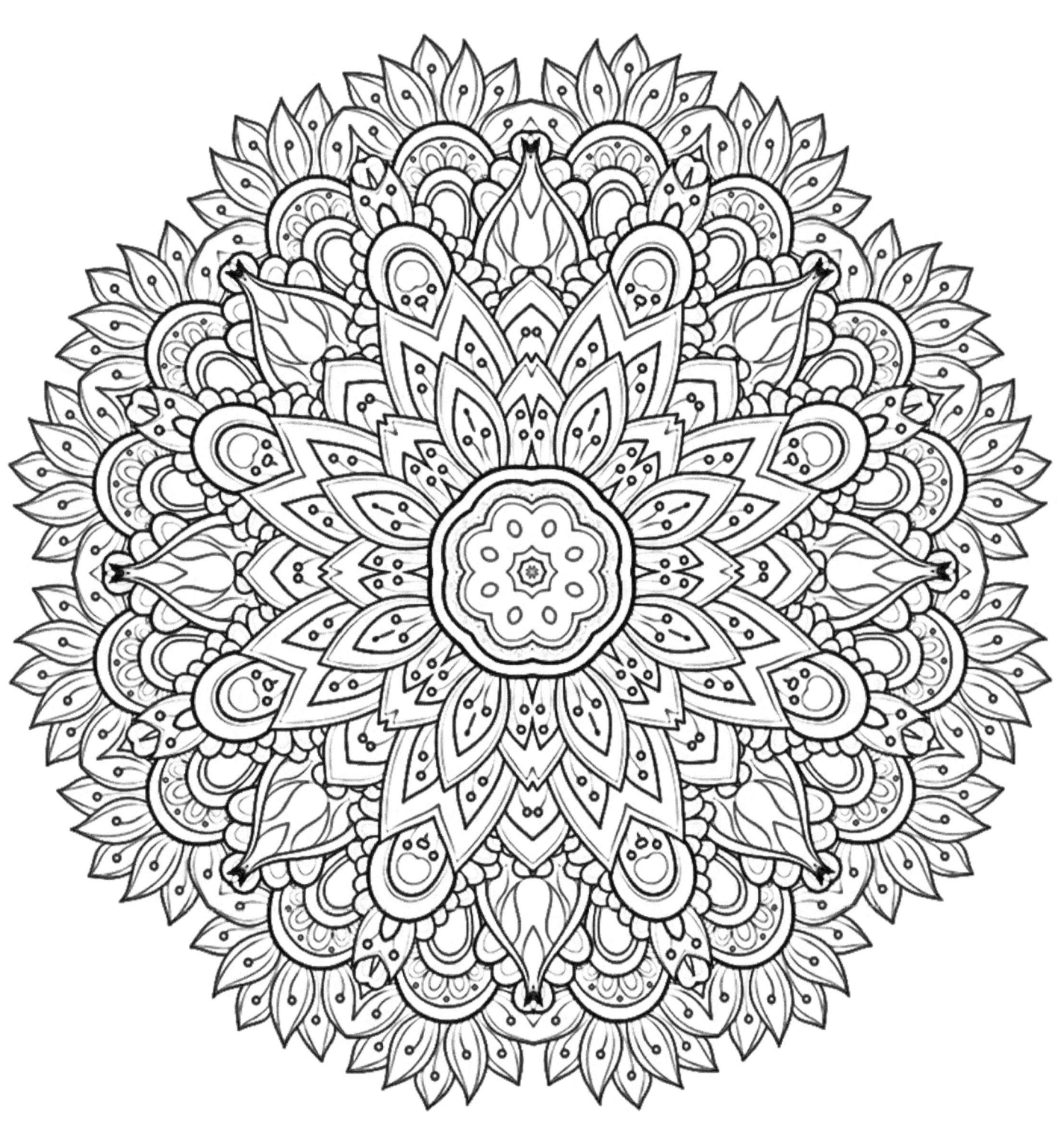

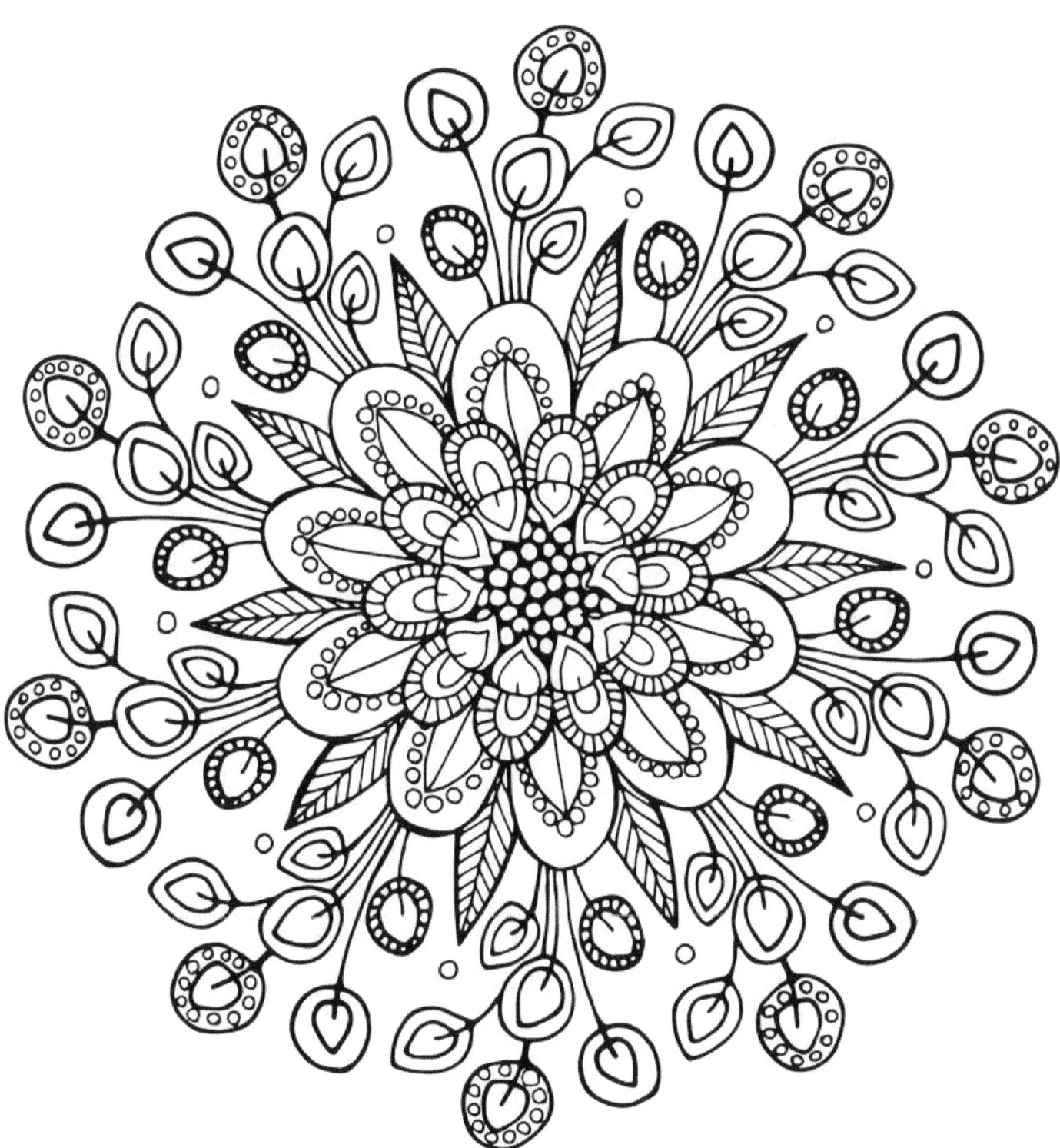

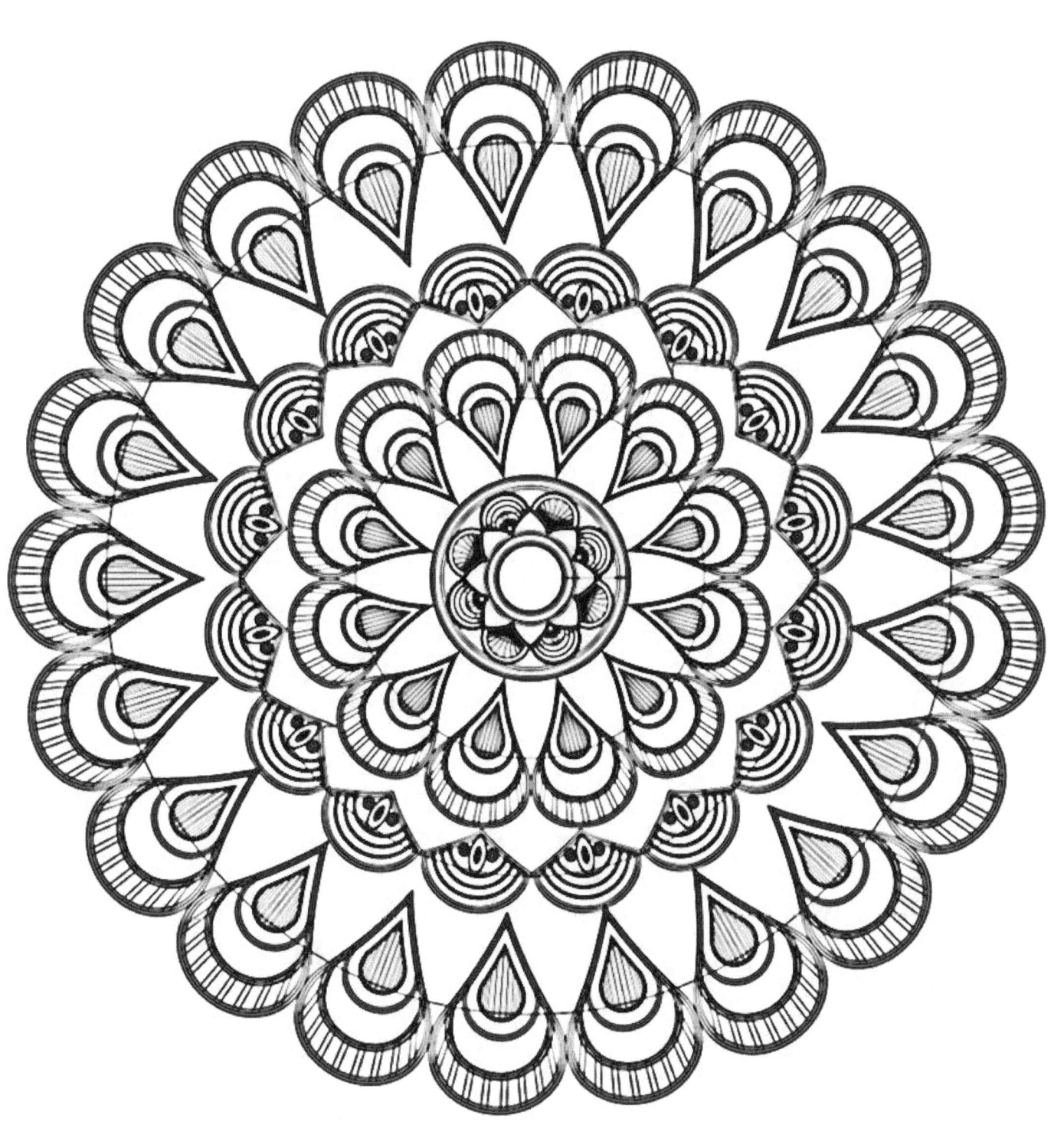

www.ingramcontent.com/pod-product-compliance
Lightning Source LLC
Chambersburg PA
CBHW080959220526
45467CB00008B/2626